MAYAN VISION QUEST

MAYAN VISION QUEST

MYSTICAL INITIATION IN MESOAMERICA

PHOTOGRAPHS BY CYNTHIA MACADAMS

TEXT BY HUNBATZ MEN AND CHARLES BENSINGER

HarperSanFrancisco

A Division of HarperCollins*Publishers*

Frontispiece:
During the spring and fall equinoxes, the sun casts shadows in the shape of seven isosceles triangles on the side of this pyramid, known as El Castillo (or the Pyramid of Kukulcan). This astronomical event symbolizes the return of the feathered serpent deity, known as Kukulcan. (*Chichén Itzá*)

For Mayan Vision Quest, *I used Nikon FM and FE2 cameras with Nikon lenses to capture the mystical forces in the pyramids and temples. My favorite lens is the macro-55. I used infrared film ninety percent of the time and T-max ten percent of the time. Infrared Kodak film set at 100 ASA with a 25A red filter gave me energized white trees and inky black skies. In using infrared film, I felt connected to the Mayan soul. Before photographing, I would meditate at the site with my cameras in hand or near my body. I would then observe the sun move from east to west, casting its changing shadows across the pyramids.* Mayan Vision Quest *is my shaman's journey into the Mayan heart.*
—*Cynthia MacAdams*

SPANISH TRANSLATION BY LOUISE MONTEZ

MAYAN VISION QUEST: *Mystical Initiation in Mesoamerica.* Copyright © 1991 by Cynthia MacAdams, Hunbatz Men, and Charles Bensinger. All rights reserved. Printed in Hong Kong. No part of this book may be used or reproduced in any manner whatsoever without written permission except in the case of brief quotations embodied in critical articles and reviews. For information, address HarperCollins Publishers, 10 East 53rd Street, New York, NY 10022.

FIRST EDITION

Library of Congress Cataloging-in-Publication Data

Hunbatz Men,
    Mayan vision quest : mystical initiation in Mesoamerica / photographs by Cynthia MacAdams ; text by Hunbatz Men and Charles Bensinger. — 1st ed.
        p.   cm.
    ISBN 0–06–250527–0. — ISBN 0–06–250565–3 (pbk.)
    1. Mayas—Religion and mythology—Miscellanea. 2. Mayas—Antiquities—Pictorial works.   3. Initiation rites—Miscellanea. 4. Occultism. 5. Spiritualism. I. MacAdams, Cynthia.   II. Bensinger, Charles. III. Title.
BF1999.H914   1991
299'.784—dc20   90–55789
                                                CIP

91 92 93 94 94 HCP-HK 10 9 8 7 6 5 4 3 2 1

CONTENTS

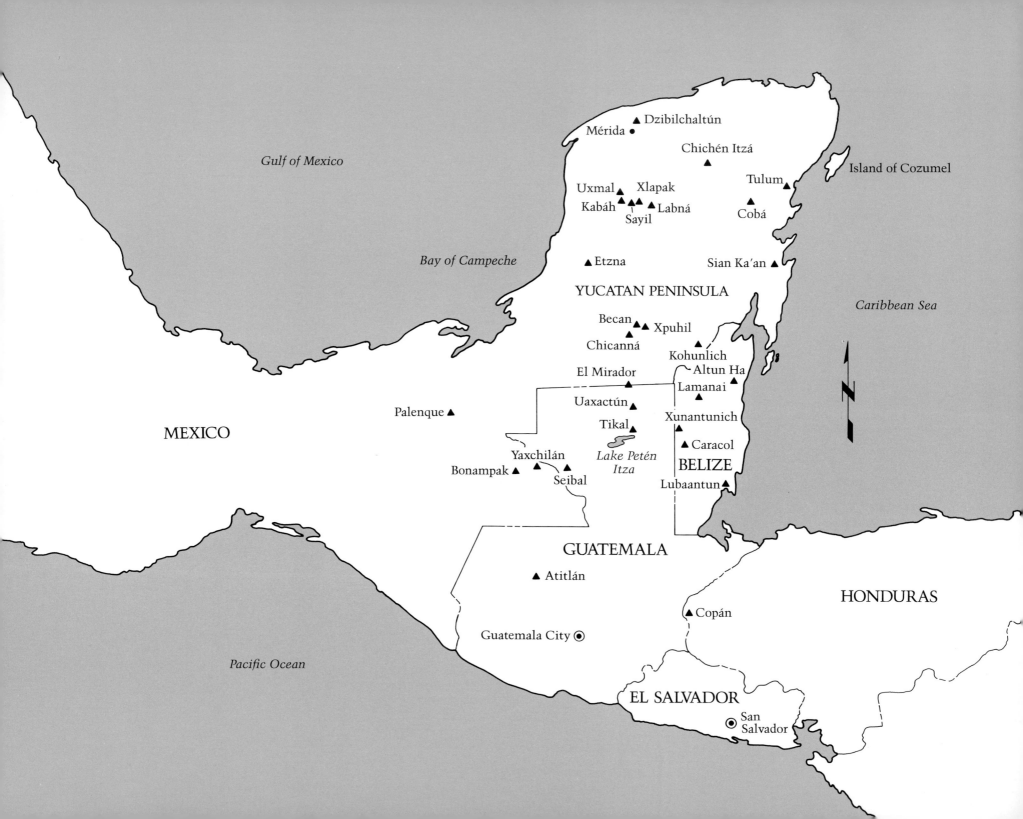

INTRODUCTION

WITH THE FOLLOWING INSIGHTFUL and prophetic words, Maya priest and shaman Hunbatz Men illuminates the enigmatic Maya and their intimate and complex kinship with the sun and its divine power source:

"The Maya call the sun *K'in*, the great generator of energy whose job it is to create harmony among all the moons and planets of our solar system. When we pray to K'in, we summon the energy of the creative life force, the transformer of all things. K'in also serves as the omnipresent, fiery lens through which the universal creative force is radiated to the planet earth providing for the nurturance and continuance of all life. The Maya know this divine force as *Hunab K'U*, the One Giver of Movement and Measure.

"Hunab K'U, the supreme principle of the cosmic teaching, is now reminding us to renew again the ceremonial centers of the Maya wherein resides the universal wisdom. This knowledge can be found in the sacred places of Mexico, Guatemala, Belize, Honduras, and El Salvador where stand the great pyramids and temples of old. From these timeless centers of knowledge, the voices of the ancient ones will begin to emanate from the rocks, the glyphs, and the geometry of our jungle-enshrouded cities. Here we will learn to communicate again with the natural forces of creation.

"For many centuries the initiates of the world traveled here from distant countries to study with the Maya solar priests. On sacred Maya earth, there once stood Babylonians, Tibetans, Peruvians, and representatives from many cultures—all to partake of this cosmic knowledge.

"The ancient Maya centers evoked the admiration of many civilizations throughout the world for thousands of years. But one day, the people began to forget their commitment to the sacred song of creation and the cosmic cycles of time. As a result, a long, dark shadow of fear and violence fell upon our land, causing great spiritual pain and damping for many centuries the bright-burning light of cosmic and universal knowledge. But the Maya sages foresaw that with the passage of time, people would return to the land of the Maya to regain the knowledge of these ageless stones, which now vibrate to a new era. They knew that some day men and women would teach that which was written here by the ancient Maya priests and priestesses in order to aid humanity in its time of crisis.

"The Maya Prophecies say that now the time has come to relearn and remember the deepest universal truths. Hunab K'U desires to reawaken our conscious and unconscious selves in order that we may discover our true and highest human potential."

The Maya viewed science as inseparable from spiritual cosmology. Consequently, they developed ingenious means of interpreting the universal web of causation and applying it to their daily life.

The Maya were endlessly fascinated with the cycles

of time, and they viewed the movement of all things in the cosmos as hooked to time. To comprehend time and movement was to know God and the Galactic Mind. They used this knowledge to chart the past and predict the future. As accomplished navigators, familiar with plane and spherical trigonometry, they computed the size of the world, estimated the distance from pole to pole, and calculated the length of a meridian. They may have regularly sailed to India, Egypt, and many distant lands. Like the Egyptians and other highly sophisticated cultures of antiquity, the Maya designed their buildings, especially their pyramids, to embody their physical and spiritual relationship to the cosmos. Certain hieroglyphic inscriptions record important dates or events that occurred some four hundred million years ago. Maya astronomers managed calculations of astounding complexity using only three types of notation—a bar, a dot, and a shell glyph or zero.

This unique body of inquiry and wisdom is reflected in the world's most elaborate system of calendars, a grand style of ritual and ceremony, a highly developed language, an advanced intensive form of agriculture, and a knowledge of geometry and architecture that produced some of the most exquisite temples and pyramids found anywhere in the world.

The Maya developed an ingenious means of recording their vital knowledge in exotic inscriptions called *hieroglyphs*. These visual-phonetic iconographs or carved descriptive narratives told of the powerful interactions of the Maya gods and goddesses and the makeup of the Maya cosmos. They also depicted calendric and mythical time and agricultural cycles, served as a catalog of important dynastic events, and recorded the ritual and daily life of royalty.

Hunbatz Men states that "a new reign of human enlightenment will commence, according to the prophecies, in the year A.D. 2013. At this time, the first stage of higher understanding will begin. If we are willing to work with our subconscious, we will then be able to reclaim the information that has been impregnated in the deepest parts of our being. In this way, the ancient knowledge will rise again, reminding us of the remote time in which humanity was of one mind and spoke with a single symbolic, mantric, and scientific idiom."

The Maya sacred centers can serve as powerful catalysts for this work. As archeologist John Steele has said, "Sacred sites serve to wake us up. They remind us to *remember to remember*" (from the video "Geomancy, East and West" by Joan Price, Santa Fe: Video Southwest, 1991). Sacred sites can jog our sometimes arthritic consciousness into taking bold and magical action. And this, indeed, is the purpose of the vision quest and the process of initiation—to undertake the personal, transformative experience. The vision seeker is aspiring to gain insights into things deeply hidden, perhaps to probe the hazy memories of past lives or discover ways of viewing contemporary reality in a new, revealing light. It's the mythical journey of the archetypal "hero" or "heroine." It's an inner voyage that demands more the faculties of trust and intuition than the powers of the intellectual mind.

Anyone with sufficient motivation can undertake a vision quest. But such cosmic communion cannot be approached casually. The seeker must be prepared to undergo an often wrenching process of personal change and transformation, a kind of *rite of passage*. A rite of passage implies a distinct movement from one stage of awareness to another. Persons electing to pursue such experiences permanently are known in spiritual schools as *initiates*, and the process is usually termed an *initiation*.

During initiation, the participant embarks on a journey to explore the realms of the normally unknowable—that which is secret and hidden. The ordinary ebb and flow of the mundane world is left behind, and the goal becomes the realization of the wholeness of existence. Journeying into such territories, where powerful forces reside, requires total commitment. One must be willing to surrender the ego self and be prepared to undergo metaphoric death and rebirth.

Maya rituals and temples were designed to evoke and facilitate this potent experiential process, and regular vision questing was a common feature of Maya religious practice. In classic period Maya art we find scenes that depict royalty performing various kinds of personal bloodletting rituals to gain visions. The Maya generally focused on communication with specific ancestors, gods, and animal spirits, depicting the results of this process through the image of the *vision serpent*. The vision serpent is an undulating, highly stylized serpent figure from whose gaping jaws emerged the face of the object of the invocation: a royal ancestor, a long-dead warrior, or some other being resident in the nether world. Classic period temple lintels, stucco panels, and stone carvings frequently depict the vision serpent apparition suspended above the man or woman engaged in the vision-producing rite. This rite usually involved ceremoniously piercing specific parts of the body, commonly the tongue for women and the penis for men, in order to shed blood and induce an altered state of consciousness. Intimate discourse with the supernatural world then became possible and was, in fact, considered crucial to the perpetuation of Maya society.

In contemporary times, we have even greater need for such journeying into source and causal realities. Indeed, our world cries out for expansive, novel visioning to enable us to successfully meet the trying challenges of the decades ahead. As truly alive human beings, we long for the experience of the supernatural, the mythic, and the ecstatic where we may enter sacred space, merge with the profound, and come to know the sanctity and wholeness of life in all its beauty.

Is it possible that twentieth-century pilgrims seeking such insights, too, may make use of the knowledge of the ancient Maya to aid in a contemporary quest for universal truth and wisdom? Do the silent stones of the ancient Maya ceremonial centers still hold secrets that might be revealed to the open and sensitive visitor? Will the spirits commune with those who come to truly listen?

An essential key that serves to unlock the gates to parallel worlds is an attitude of respectful intention and an active willingness to invite the spirits of place to communicate freely and in whatever way is appropriate. Anything, then, becomes possible. The thin veil of present-time reality may suddenly part, and voices unknown will join with jungle chatter. Trees, animals, stones, and sky can become informants containing a consciousness of their own. Shapes unreal may flutter about seemingly empty temple vaults and dark, lifeless corridors. Messages are delivered. Visions occur. A burning question is answered. The pilgrim's quest is acknowledged.

COPÁN

Ever watchful, this demigod figure holds the sacred serpent in his mouth, symbolizing the wisdom of one initiated into Maya serpent culture. His imposing presence reminds all who enter into this sacred ceremonial space of the everpresent guardianship of the gods. (*Copán*)

THE COPÁN EMBLEM GLYPH means "place of the clouds." Gentle and mysterious, half-hidden in the rainy mist, the great city of Copán exudes a sense of rarefied grace and classic elegance. The city's location on the Río Copán, just inside Honduras near the Guatemala border, places it on an ancient trade route that led from the Pacific Coast to the Montagua River. At its height, ten thousand people lived in and around this majestic governmental and ceremonial center.

A huge human-made mountain of stone blocks covers within its bulk three generations of ancient cities, each one overlaid upon the other. The towering, multilayered acropolis served as a center of government—a kind of Maya congress. Delegates would travel here to pay homage to powerful leaders and exchange thoughts about politics, science, and religion. A palpable sense of confidence hangs in the humid afternoon air. One can detect here the presence of wisdom gained by long centuries of trial and error, of critical knowledge laboriously transported from distant places.

Copán's precise symmetrical pyramids, the intentional sacred spaces defined by its grand courtyards, and the inventive special features such as the exotic Hieroglyphic Stairway attest to an architectual and design genius stunning in its manifestation. The Copán ball court, though small but classical in style and shape and situated centrally in the grand plaza, vividly recalls the secular and spiritual importance of the ball game that was the most famous of all public rituals in Mesoamerica.

In the past, Copán served as a science center, too. Astronomers, astrologers, mathematicians, and calendar priests convened here for conferences and symposia. The best mathematical minds of the times would set about the imposing tasks of refining the complex Mayan Calendar, designing ever better star charts and defining the interactions of the celestial clockwork with human destiny.

Within and about the wide plazas and courtyards stand vertical stone monuments or *stelae*. These elaborately carved three-dimensional sculptures feature important personages bedecked in attire rich with fantastic symbology linking the wearer to the highest cosmic forces. The old Maya rulers of Copán seem to pose as silent observers, their larger-than-life stone images appearing almost as alive today as they were twelve hundred years ago. A visitor to ancient

Copán would arrive in the grand plaza, pass these huge, dramatic figures, and encounter the elaborate Hieroglyphic Stairway rising steeply into the sky. Four otherworldly half-human, half-animal creatures awaited at intervals beside the glyph-covered steps. At the top of the pyramid's lofty summit, the visitor would greet the current ruler, seated in the temple upon a richly adorned throne. No one could fail to be profoundly impressed by the grandeur and power of this exotic setting.

The larger-than-life visages of the stelae haunt the quiet plaza in the company of their nearby pyramid guardians. These human figures, so realistically carved, almost ask for release, as if they were indeed truly flesh and bone, only temporarily trapped in stone. The onlooker is tempted to clasp hands across twelve centuries of separation, perhaps to bind together the knowledge of both our worlds in time. It seems the ancient ones still remain a part of us—their energies somehow faintly resident in our human cells—calling out to us from hidden memories and quietly speaking to us through our dreams.

Stela C (A.D. 782) depicts a young man dressed in elaborate attire composed of various planetary and terrestrial symbols. Monkey god and sun god faces symbolize powerful spiritual entities invoked to aid the wearer during his journey through the physical life and beyond into the afterlife. (*Copán*)

3

4

The ball game played in this ball court (A.D. 775) recalls the ancient myth of the hero twins Hunahpu and Xbalanque from the important postclassic book *Popol Vuh*. This sacred text describes how the hero twins became drawn into a deadly supernatural ball game in *Xibalba* (the underworld) with the underworld gods. The hero twins were repeatedly confronted with impossible and fatal challenges. (*Copán*) ◄

Called "one of the great ancient architectural achievements of the world," the Hieroglyphic Stairway contains the longest body of Maya inscriptions—more than twenty-five hundred individual glyphs. It is believed that Copán's fifteenth ruler, Smoke Shell, constructed the stairway in the eighth century to commemorate the dynastic history of Copán's rulers with a particular emphasis placed on the glorious reign of Copán's twelfth ruler, Smoke Imix God K. The ancient visitor to Copán seeking audience with the ruler would ascend these broad steps and enter a royal receiving room inside the pyramid's summit temple. (*Copán*) ►

During special calendrical periods, the sacred ball game called *pok-ta-pok* was played here in the ball court to symbolically recall the supernatural origins of the Maya and the relationship of the Maya physical world to the movement of the celestial bodies. (*Copán*) ◄

This small pyramid was used to offer tribute and to petition the deities for permission to make important personal life changes. (*Copán*) ►

Symbolic of the underworld, a Cauac Monster head on the altar zoomorph for Stela D is surrounded by various metaphysical symbols. These striking images remind the petitioner of the powerful and threatening presence of the underworld and its various wrathful deities. For the Maya, the continuance of life depended on the proper acknowledgment of these fierce and dangerous underworld forces. (*Copán*)

The Venus Altar is in the Eastern Court. Nearby, in the Temple of Meditations, is a special window that may have been used for astronomical study of the cycles of Venus. (*Copán*)

In the Venus Plaza and on the Jaguar Stairway in the Eastern Court, important ceremonial activities were held to honor Venus as it led the sun out of the underworld. The first reappearance of Venus often signaled a period of renewed Maya warfare. (*Copán*) ◄

The Maya consider the massive, towering ceiba tree as the sacred Tree of Life or *axis mundi*, the center of the world. The tree represents the links between the separate levels of the cosmos: its roots descend into the underworld, its trunk stands in the middleworld, and its branches reach high into the heavens, or upperworld. Tree or cross symbology appears frequently in Maya art. The tree is also revered as the sustainer of life because of its critical role in the atmospheric rain cycle. The Maya say: "From this tree the first human emerged. . . . With the death of the last tree comes the death of the last human." (*Copán*) ►

Pyramid 4 (A.D. 731) stands in the center of the main plaza. It was used for a wide variety of ceremonial and ritual purposes. (*Copán*)

In this temple overlooking the ball court, priests and rulers would gather to discuss the ball game, an important public ritual that reminded participants and spectators alike of the Maya multidimensional relationship among the underworld, the surface or middleworld, and the celestial world. (*Copán*)

Stela A (A.D. 731) is a portrait of the thir-
teenth ruler of Copán, known as 18 Rabbit.
He holds his doubleheaded serpent bar,
which displays twin Sun gods on each side.
The mat symbols above his head mark him
as royalty. On his belt hang bags of sting-
ray spines used for ritual bloodletting rites
commonly practiced by the Maya elite.
Facial images of important deities attest to
18 Rabbit's invocation of cosmic powers.
Stela records seem to indicate that 18 Rabbit was captured and beheaded by the ruler
of the nearby Maya city of Quirigua.
(*Copán*)

On Stela P (A.D. 623), the oldest stela of Copán, a male ruler is accompanied by numerous deities such as the Jester God, Serpent God, Ahau Sun God, and Jaguar God. The Maya believed that the physical depiction through symbol of these important gods drew to the bearer the god's unique power, wisdom, and guidance. (*Copán*)

UAXACTÚN
SEIBAL
TIKAL
EL MIRADOR
ATITLÁN

These ruins lie a day's walk north of the great Maya center of Tikal. Here priests, priestesses, and initiates performed the necessary meditations, purification rituals, and ceremonies required by the dictates of spiritual custom. (*Uaxactún*)

DEEP WITHIN THE LUSH PETÉN lowland jungle forest of Guatemala hide mysterious stone time machines. The grand pyramids of El Mirador and Tikal scrape the blue tropical sky, while farther south, majestic Lake Atitlán reflects a towering volcano and the old city of Seibal hugs the banks of the Río Pasión.

A medium-sized ceremonial center, Seibal served as a meeting place for traders and adventurers traveling throughout the vast Maya empire. In Seibal, an ambient sense of expectation remains, perhaps echoing old memories of exchanged rare goods and expert storytelling. Such elusive traces of the past seem to float suspended beneath the towering, moisture-dripping ceiba trees.

TIKAL

In the central Petén forest, the huge city of Tikal rises imposingly. Nearby is its smaller companion city, Uaxactún, also a spectacular ceremonial center.

Tikal during its heyday must have been extraordinary. At its height (A.D. 600–900) possibly as many as fifty thousand people resided within the fifty square miles of jungle that comprised one of the oldest and largest of ancient Maya urban centers.

Ridiculously steep, thrusting their massive roof combs through the humid jungle canopy, Tikal's pyramids evoke a sense of otherworldy wonder. What strangely inventive minds could have conjured up such rich visions of space and form and so skillfully expressed them in vertical and horizontal stone?

Tikal, like other major Maya cities, functioned as a governmental, educational, economic, scientific, and ceremonial center. Embodied in its pyramids are calendric computations and other notations of Maya religious/scientific study whose purpose was to link the Maya's daily life to the cyclic machinations of the cosmos. Visitors would journey from afar to gather here, to make offerings of sacred objects, receive initiations, and celebrate the occurrence of important calendar cycles and celestial events.

Powerful ruler-priests with exotic names like Jaguar Paw, Curl Nose, Stormy Sky, Shield Skull, and Half-Darkened Sun directed Tikal's destiny. Now they rest in silence within their richly decorated tombs of stone; perhaps their ghosts admire the stares of wonder on the faces of awed visitors pondering the mysterious enchantment of these steep-walled pyramids and intriguing multilevel temples.

Howler monkeys scream their way through the jungle, sweeping the Central Acropolis in mid-afternoon, just as they did when Curl Nose or Stormy Sky presided over this imposing masonry metropolis. Keel-billed toucans, parrots, and motmots glide past jungle-choked stone monuments as if on patrols commissioned by some unseen ancient guardians.

One interpretation of the word *tikal* is "the place where the cycles of cosmic time remain registered." Within the inner chambers of Tikal's temples and pyramids, Maya priests and priestesses would study and practice advanced scientific and spiritual knowledge. Here the Maya also created specialized botanical gardens and laboratories, often using certain pyramids to channel biomagnetic energies into selected plants. From these experiments, they created a sophisticated science of genetic engineering.

Pilgrims bearing gifts and sacred offerings no longer travel the ancient white roadways to Tikal. Yet powerful energies remain within and about this great Maya center. Much knowledge is stored in the stones and the ethers awaiting the respectful and sensitive student. Invisible gatekeepers/teachers wait patiently as they have for so many centuries. They stand by in confidence, knowing that as their calendar predicts, the inevitable cycle of reemergence will someday soon summon forth a new flourishing of life, learning, and celebration to fill Tikal's pyramids and plazas with voice, prayer, and ceremony once again.

From this Jaguar Temple platform (stela in foreground), the priests would observe the sun during the solar equinoxes and solstices as it rose behind the triple temple complex directly across the plaza. (*Uaxactún*)

19

Three ghostly temple platforms known as Group E mark the solstice and equinox cycles. At the spring and fall equinoxes (March 21 and September 23), the sun rises directly behind the center temple. At the summer and winter solstices (June 21 and December 21), the sun rises behind the temple on the left and the temple on the right, respectively. (*Uaxactún*)

Resplendent Maya solar priests would stand upon this temple platform to observe the sun during the equinoxes and solstices as it rose behind one of the three pyramid-temples situated in the background. The stela in the foreground is aligned with the three stelae in front of the center equinox temple, allowing precise calibration of the astronomical event. (*Uaxactún*)

The Temple of the Masks (Structure E-VII-Sub.) is a late preclassic structure showing stairways on all four sides flanked by tiers of stucco god masks. This temple may have served to teach the religious importance of the number twenty, the basis of the Mayan Calendar system. (*Uaxactún*) ◄

In this temple room containing a stela and altar, Maya sun priests received initiates arriving to take instruction in the sacred mysteries. Here the initiates would learn of the responsibility of the solar man to his community. Major activities of the Uaxactún center included the worship of the solar forces. (*Uaxactún*) ►

This stela embodies important symbols used for special instruction of priests and priestesses. Lunar observations and agricultural research were important areas of inquiry pursued in the temples, fields, and forests of Seibal. (*Seibal*)

Situated along the Río Pasión, Seibal functioned as a major botanical research center. Here, amid thick waves of pure oxygen and abundant rainfall generated by Seibal's dense forest, medicinal herbs and special plant cultivation techniques were studied with great intensity. (*Seibal*)

An intriguing labyrinth of doorways, rooms, and private temples suggests this complex served as a kind of university for the investigation of the mystical arts. The ancient curriculum possibly included the investigation of calendric relationships; the hidden powers of intuition, *kundalini* (sexual energy) and human sexuality; multidimensional levels of awareness; out-of-body travel; and other aspects of esoteric knowledge. (*Tikal*)

Many stelae and their accompanying altars grace the broad Great Plaza. These stelae honor Tikal's important rulers and their relatives, special ritual events in Tikal's history, and important calendar cycles. (*Tikal*)

The round rock in the foreground served as an altar where flowers and sacred objects were placed as offerings. On the summit platforms of the pyramid-temples overlooking this Great Plaza, priests, priestesses, and noble personages would assemble to witness the colorful pageantry conducted in the plaza below. The conspicuous presence of the Maya elite thus assured Tikal's residents that the critical relationship between the human world and the divine world remained in perfect balance. (*Tikal*) ◄

Multiple room blocks, interior temple platforms, and mysterious passageways suggest that the Central Acropolis was once home to a large body of student initiates pursuing the study of cosmic science and other sacred arts. (*Tikal*) ►

This aerial view of the Great Plaza of Tikal shows the Temple of the Masks and the Central and North acropoli. For many centuries, this great city served as a kind of spiritual mecca, governmental focal point, and major educational, ceremonial, scientific, and trade center. (*Tikal*)

Quietly brooding over the Great Plaza, the Temple of the Giant Jaguar stands ever watchful. Pilgrims would place their offerings and sacred objects on round altars honoring deceased rulers, elevated after death to ancestral deities. (*Tikal*)

On this early classic Chac (rain god) mask in North Acropolis, the ears are symbolic of the spirit, and the mouth and oversized nose represent wind or the breath of life. One of the most important Mesoamerican deities, the rain god governed water, the cleansing elements of nature and human fluids as well. (*Tikal*)

The Temple of the Giant Jaguar is framed by the doorway of the Temple of the Masks. Pyramids were often aligned and designed to facilitate perfect voice transmission between the summits and the plazas below. (*Tikal*) ▶

Stela 22 (A.D. 771) is framed by an arch at Complex Q. This area is part of a twin pyramid complex intended to celebrate one *katun,* a twenty-year calendar period. Special ceremonies would be held in these areas to officially recognize the pattern of cosmic order as expressed through cyclic and historical time periods. (*Tikal*)

The Temple of the Masks was painted in accordance with certain cyclical changes as determined by Maya scientific and religious knowledge. To enhance the rituals performed here, colors were changed to ensure the optimum energy flow through the structure. (*Tikal*)

Hidden beneath the lush growth of rainforest lie more than three thousand structures including some two hundred stone monuments. Temples can be found distributed widely throughout the jungle, suggesting that the Maya considered this style of architecture and its subsequent function to be of great spiritual and pragmatic importance to their society. (*Tikal*)

The Temple of the Giant Jaguar, built in approximately A.D. 700 by Ah Cacaw, was designed to dramatically convey to the community of Tikal the power of its ruler-builder as well as the spiritual relationship between human and cosmos. Calendric knowledge revealing the solar cycles and their effect on human life and natural systems was encoded and disseminated here as well. (*Tikal*)

The Temple of the Masks stands silent and proud, flanked by other nearby pyramids, stately roof combs thrusting beyond the jungle's insistent reach. Some no doubt journeyed to Tikal because of exotic tales recounted at a distant campfire by a talkative bard. Others traveled here regularly to petition the gods and the goddesses for divine intercession and to offer sacred objects in acknowledgment of granted favors. (*Tikal*) ◀

The temples and stelae in the North Acropolis serve as a series of monuments dedicated to deceased and now deified royal ancestors. (*Tikal*) ▶

This palace structure and altar stones are found in the older, preclassic section of Tikal. Often such round stones were used as recording devices to store information pertaining to the design and purpose of the nearby pyramid. The information could then be released again by appropriate ritual and ceremony. Mystic Edgar Cayce referred to large round stones as Atlantean remains that, used as altars, could cleanse human bodies of such undesirable qualities as hate, malice, and self-indulgence. Special initiates would channel powerful healing energies into the bodies of the afflicted person prostrate upon the stone. (*Tikal*) ◄

This ceremonial complex was designated to honor a particular purpose such as a calendar cycle, a significant historical event, or an important personage or deity. (*Tikal*) ►

Like indestructible giants awakening from the slumber of centuries, Maya pyramids rise from the American jungle, recalling an earlier era of ancient empire and the amazing achievements of a civilization almost unparalleled in history. (*Tikal*)

42

The Great Pyramid of the Sun reposes gracefully in the Lost World Pyramid Complex. Everywhere throughout the Petén jungle can be found grand, human-made structures whose design and construction still conceal many secrets of Maya cosmic knowledge. (*Tikal*)

The Watchtower is one of the highest Maya pyramids and is nearly inaccessible by land. In the past, ancient roads connected El Mirador to Tikal. From the pyramid's summit one can appreciate the immensity of the spectacular jungle and the determination and creativity of the remarkable people who settled here. (*El Mirador*)

A towering volcano overlooks Lake Atitlán. Maya fishermen settled around the lake and developed fish and shellfish hatcheries in order to trade with the larger population in the Maya urban centers. (*Lake Atitlán*) ▶

PALENQUE
YAXCHILÁN
BONAMPAK

Deep inside the beautiful Temple of the Inscriptions can be found the tomb of the greatly esteemed Maya ruler and priest, Lord Pacal, interred here in A.D. 683. The lid above his sarcophagus contains an elaborate carving of the sacred Tree of Life absorbing Pacal into its roots, drawing him into the underworld. A stone breathing tube connecting Pacal's tomb to the temple on the summit of the pyramid allowed Pacal to communicate with the living as he traveled into the afterlife. The nine pyramid levels symbolize the nine layers of the Maya underworld. (*Palenque*)

IN THE STATE OF CHIAPAS, Mexico, near the Usumacinta River, a critical Maya transportation waterway, rises a steep ridge of lush rainforest. Below this rainforest stretches a wide, fertile valley fed by abundant rains. The Maya, knowing the potential of a rich natural environment, chose to locate their exquisite city of Palenque here on a commanding site overlooking the placid valley below.

Many regard Palenque as the most beautiful, elegant, and evocative of all ancient Maya ceremonial centers. Its lightness and grace as portrayed through its structures bear proud tribute to its master architects. Unlike other Maya temples, the vaults and doorways at Palenque are spacious and inviting. Palenque is filled with expressive stuccoed bas-reliefs depicting scenes of ritual and dynastic history that have no parallel elsewhere in the ancient world. Palenque exudes an air of carefully timed withholding, of barely concealed secret knowledge drifting just beyond the accessible level of physical reality, tantalizing the seeker of such things. Palenque, to the observant, is clearly a repository of powerful and guarded mystic knowledge.

Certain of Palenque's temples served as study centers emphasizing the significance of the cross, an important Maya symbol of human evolution. Astronomical observations were carried out from the seven-story palace tower, perhaps using crystal technologies.

Palenque prospered as the foremost center of the westernmost sector of the Maya world under the guidance of Lord Pacal. His richly arrayed tomb deep within the beautiful Temple of the Inscriptions became one of the greatest finds in the history of American archeology. This discovery by Alberto Ruz Lhuiller in 1952 revealed a magnificently carved sarcophagus lid and a large cache of precious jade objects.

There also exist provocative indications that Palenque may be the "mysterious city of the south," or *Ba-lat-quah-bi*, the origin city of the Hopi Indians of the southwestern United States. Specific characteristics of Palenque fit easily into Hopi descriptions of the legendary city, and wall inscriptions depict imagery reminiscent of Hopi artifacts and designs. Numerous elements of Hopi ritual, language, and spiritual history suggest strong Hopi-Maya links in the past.

What we know of Palenque seems to hint of incredible goings-on here in the fastness of this tropical jungle sanctuary. A walk into the surrounding forest plunges the visitor into a lost world, root-entangled stairways tripping one's every step, unexpected stone walls emerging from eroding stream banks. Time seems to stop and reverse, the heavens shift, and the ever-raucous jungle chatter lapses easily into a mysterious parenthesis of silence. One can almost sense that Palenque could become alive again, filled with human voices and the clatter of a busy community.

YAXCHILÁN AND BONAMPAK

Further inland along the Usumacinta River can be found the cities of Yaxchilán and Bonampak. Both these settlements contain artful stelae and hieroglyphs and colorful murals depicting vivid scenes of Maya life. Unique to Yaxchilán are portrayals of women on relief sculptures, indicating important social and spiritual roles. These exquisite carvings feature royal men and women engaged in mind-altering bloodletting rituals and celebrating important moments in dynastic history.

Bonampak is famous for the finest surviving murals in the New World and stone carvings of wonderful detail describing court and battle scenes. Such masterful artwork, now more than a thousand years old, allows us a glimpse into a culture both intensely creative and wildly provocative.

The Temple of the Foliated Cross taught the importance of the constellation of the Southern Cross, visible in the heavens during May of each year. The tree, too, symbolized the relationship between the physical and cosmic worlds. Inside the temple superb relief sculptures carved on limestone tablets record the accession to the throne of the ruler Chan Bahlum. (*Palenque*)

The Grand Palace (A.D. 720) served as a residence for important personages and initiates studying the sacred arts. The seven-level tower, an astronomical observatory, is similar in design to the King's Chamber in the Great Pyramid of Egypt. Both structures suggest a spiritual purpose, as most esoteric traditions require the seeker to undergo a seven-step process of initiation. (*Palenque*) ◄

The Grand Palace complex contains many tunnels and subterranean passageways that were used by initiates studying Maya esoteric traditions. Stucco reliefs inside the palace depict Maya deities and scenes of individual empowerment. Crystals found in the palace tower may have been used as tools for astronomical study or mystical investigation. (*Palenque*) ►

Constructed in A.D. 642, the Temple of the
Sun is distinguished by its fine roof comb
and delicate, well-balanced proportions.
Inside the temple a relief panel shows a
seated ruler-priest holding a ceremonial
bar and surrounded by deities. (*Palenque*)

In the Temple of the Foliated Cross we find an excellent example of the classic Maya corbeled arch. Intriguing stucco scenes in the interior of the temple depict important ritual events that occurred in Palenque more than a thousand years ago. (*Palenque*)

The corbeled arch near the palace complex suggests that many sacred places of worship and study are contained within and around this structure. (*Palenque*)

It is said that this Maya profile is characteristic of people who traveled to the Yucatan from Atlantis following that continent's submergence many millennia ago. Ancient Maya texts describe the first inhabitants of the Yucatan as arriving by boat from the east after a great flood. (*Palenque*)

A major city with large pyramids situated along the Usumacinta River,
Yaxchilán featured an impressive ceremonial center with powerful royal
dynasties. Superb carved lintels depict vision quest rituals practiced by ruler Bird
Jaguar and his wife, Lady Xoc. (*Yaxchilán*)

Wind passing through the elaborate roof comb apertures on this temple would produce harmonious sounds in the temple area, reproducing the voices of the gods. (*Yaxchilán*)

This stone relief shows an angry Maya warrior accompanied by symbols denoting the cycles of time. (*Bonampak*)

In Bonampak and elsewhere, Maya architects and builders constructed pyramids into the hills in order to channel the natural energy forces in the earth into their structures. (*Bonampak*) ▶

UXMAL
AND VICINITY

In the dry country of the Yucatan, much depended on the favorable intercession of Chac, the rain god. Consequently, Chac masks are common on Uxmal's stone facades. Prayers and entreaties to Chac often served as the core of Maya rituals. (*Uxmal*)

THE VISITOR IS USUALLY NOT prepared for Uxmal's sensational impact. The huge bulk of the gently rounded Pyramid of the Magician (or Soothsayer) is the first structure encountered along the entrance path to the site. Its sharply rising stairway seems almost too steep to climb. Its soft curves reflect a sensitivity to form, shadow, and esthetics that must deeply impress the most jaded of pyramid aficionados.

Uxmal's spectacular temples, courtyards, plazas, long walls, and facades are jammed with mosaic stone designs featuring dizzying geometric shapes and tangles of turtles, fish, undulating serpents, grotesque masks, and occasional human beings. Clearly the Maya at Uxmal developed to perfection this style of using cut stone in building facades.

Slightly west of the Pyramid of the Magician, a great rectangular complex called the Nunnery Quadrangle inspires instant wonder with its simple geometric beauty, large size, and sweeping grace. Beyond lie other massive complexes of temples, causeways, and pyramids only partly wrested from the jungle's insistent grasp.

UC means "moon" in the Mayan language. Uxmal's original name was *UC-mal*, "the place of the eternal moon." Because the moon represents the power of woman and sexuality, Uxmal's many secrets have much to do with the conscious use of *kundalini* or human sexual energy. The kundalini energy is represented by the sacred snake so prevalent on Uxmal's elaborate facades.

One can easily imagine the Maya priestesses of old, dressed in their ritual clothing, descending the grand, wide staircase into the broad plaza in the Nunnery Quadrangle. Horns, drums, and flutes would summon the sacred serpent. Hearts and pulses would quicken as the gathered multitudes sensed the energy rising within them. Participants in these rites would soon begin to sense the powerful fires of inner passion rising as the tightly coiled energies stored within their bodies sought release. Women's eyes would shimmer like bright, flashing suns with the knowledge that deep inside their femaleness flowed the alchemy of ecstasy. And then the journey would commence into secret and vital dimensions.

At Uxmal women would seek to apply these sacred energies in ways that served the good of the community. They worked to bring rain, to ensure the fertility of the fields, to optimize the female-male balance and polarity, and to coax the gods and goddesses to favorably oversee the continuance of all life.

Many pyramids, temple buildings, and palace-like structures cover the dry landscape for miles around Uxmal. This network of settlements is connected by means of finely constructed roads called *sacbeob*.

In nearby Kabáh, 250 rain-god masks adorn the temple facade. As rain is always needed in this country, such magical entreaty to the gods made good practical sense. Graceful palaces at Labna and Sayil, Xpuhil, Becan, and the major ceremonial center of Etzna leave one stunned by the architectural creativity and diversity consistently expressed by Maya designers and builders.

The source of inspiration for such genius must rest in the unique synthesis of science and religion achieved by Maya priests, designers, scientists, and technicians. Over time, they managed to unravel the secrets of universal form and function, ingeniously applying these cosmic laws to the creation of structure and living environment. As observers from a very different historical era, there is much we could learn from these masters of the past that could significantly enhance the esthetics of our present-day world.

Called the Nunnery Quadrangle, this great plaza constructed in A.D. 907 served as a primary gathering place and ceremonial center. Here Maya women would practice their fertility rituals and renew their relationship with nature under the watchful gaze of the huge carved serpents that undulate across the long facades above the plaza. (*Uxmal*)

Within the Nunnery Quadrangle are seventy-four interior vaults and rooms, which at times may have served as residences for female initiates who came here to study the secrets of the natural laws that connected them to the twenty-eight-day and eighteen-year lunar cycles. (*Uxmal*) ◄

Above Uxmal's sacred ball court stand the perfectly proportioned House of the Turtles and the imposing upper pyramid complex. (*Uxmal*)

A classic stepped pyramid emerges from centuries of rubble, revealing just enough of its essence to inspire visions of richly attired priests and priestesses directing grand rituals from its steep flanks. (*Uxmal*) ◄

This aerial view of the Nunnery Quadrangle shows its broad plaza open to the sky as if seeking union with the essential elements of the heavens. Besides studying the secrets of sacred sexuality in this great initiation quadrangle, women would learn of the importance of the family unit as sustainer of the social order. (*Uxmal*) ►

The Pyramid of the Magician or Soothsayer, the only oval pyramid in the Yucatan, towers over the Nunnery Quadrangle. The pyramid contains five smaller
pyramid-temples, each superimposed over the other. Many elaborate Chac masks
and esoteric symbols adorn its front facade. (*Uxmal*)

The geometric symbols seen in this juxtaposition of the facades of the Pyramid of the Magician and a section of the Nunnery Quadrangle describe the creation of the sky and the primal forces of nature. This style of architecture, known as *Puuc*, derives its name from the low Central Yucatan mountains called the Puuc Hills. Puuc buildings typically have a plain lower facade below an ornamented upper one featuring elaborate masks and geometric designs. (*Uxmal*)

Rain god masks are surrounded by symbols depicting the nature of the cosmos. These powerful representations of deities and cosmic forces were intended to elicit a favorable response from the deities and to remind the populace of the intimate and interdependent relationship among human, deity, and cosmos. (*Uxmal*)

The crossed bones and skull speak of the human cycles of life and death. Above are hieroglyphic inscriptions that confirm the meaning of the visual symbols below. (*Uxmal*) ▶

This view of the Pyramid of the Magician or Soothsayer seems to project us into
the realm of the infinite where the ancient Maya learned to find the knowledge
they knew existed deep within themselves and their collective unconscious.
(*Uxmal*)

This dramatic archway—a classic Maya corbeled arch forming a doorway leading into the House of the Doves—indicates an entrance into a sacred area. (*Uxmal*)

As the wind moved through these specially tuned stone apertures in the House of the Doves, beautiful sounds were created in the temple area, reminding its inhabitants of the presence of the gods and the harmonious energies of nature. (*Uxmal*)

Around this special ceremonial altar recessed into the front facade of the Palace of the Governors flow symbols of the Milky Way, the planets, and various earth elements. The architecture and symbolic setting suggest a site for interdimensional communication with the sun, moon, and planets, as well as the Pleiades, Sirius, and other celestial systems. (*Uxmal*)

The Pyramid of the Magician contains teachings of Chac the rain god and his power of manifestation as administered through cyclones and hurricanes. An old legend speaks of a dwarf magician who was challenged by the Lord of Uxmal to build a temple in one night or face death. It is thought that this pyramid is his construction. (*Uxmal*)

This special temple built to honor the rain god contains a stone litany of 250 large Chac masks on its facade. Rainmaking rituals were taught here. (*Kabáh*)

The *G* symbol or spiral representing the Milky Way and the essential flow of the life force through all creation can be seen in the center of this temple. Residents here had the responsibility to study and work with these potent and important energies. (*Xlapak*)

The Palace of Sayil was built in late classic times (A.D. 800–900). With its rounded columns, unique in the Yucatan, it is clearly reminiscent of much older Greek and Egyptian architecture. Perhaps this popular classic style derives from a single, even more ancient source—the fabled continent of Atlantis. (*Sayil*)

The great corbeled arch at Labna displays serpent and celestial symbols and serves as a gateway to a sacred area. (*Labna*) ◄

From this temple situated high on a large pyramid base, stargazing Maya would observe the movement of the planets and stars, documenting critical celestial cycles in order to determine auspicious times for ceremonial events. (*Labna*) ►

A huge sculptured face of Chac, the god of thunder, lightning, and rain, adorns this dramatic entranceway, indicating that one must be willing to enter through the sometimes terrifying mouth of initiation to attain enlightenment. (*Chicanná*) ◄

An important ceremonial center and Maya marketplace situated on major trade routes, Becan's temples and plazas became busy places, rich in color, exotic activity, and on-going human drama. (*Becan*)

Soaring walls and rows of stately columns recall Xpuhil's history as an active ceremonial center. Large numbers of people participated in rituals dedicated to the sun and the cycles of nature and time. (*Xpuhil*) ◄

Here at Kohunlich is a dramatic representation of the Sun God, Kinich Ahau. A very popular and respected deity, his effigy appears frequently in Maya art and architecture. On the side are symbols of the cycles of time. (*Kohunlich*) ►

The architecture of the spectacular, multilevel pyramid-temple embodies principles of sacred geometry. Etzna's huge ceremonial plaza hosted events of elaborate pageantry involving thousands of participants and spectators. (*Etzna*)

Dzibilchaltún's origins date to 2000 B.C. Because it is one of the oldest sites of
Maya activity, its stones hold secrets stretching into the remote and distant past.
Many shells can be found buried in the ground, indicating that this area was
once covered by the ocean. (*Dzibilchaltún*)

During classic times Cobá became one of the largest urban centers in Mesoamerica and a powerful nexus of trade, residence, ceremony, and education. Special Maya roads called *sacbeob* connected Cobá to other Maya cities. From the top of this highest of Yucatan pyramids, 138 feet tall, one looks breathlessly across the vast green expanse of the table-flat Yucatan. Nearby, interrupting the forest's seamless carpet, several artificial lakes shimmer golden in the fading light of the afternoon sun. (*Cobá*) ◀

Sian Ka'an means "birth of the sky." In the upper section of this pyramid seven priests would conduct rituals to the seven solar systems. In so doing, they would renew the all-important connection between humanity and the cosmos. (*Sian Ka'an*) ▶

ALTUN HA
CARACOL
XUNANTUNICH
LAMANAI
LUBAANTUN

The Temple of the Sun God at Altun Ha was part of a powerful and dramatic religious center containing tombs of priests. Offerings of jade, copal, and resin were found near the altar here, the remains of an ancient ceremony commemorating the construction of the pyramid thirteen hundred years ago. (*Altun Ha*)

WITHIN THE LUSH TROPICAL forests of present-day Belize lie the partly excavated remains of some of the earliest known Maya settlements. Ceremonial evidence has been unearthed near the ancient cities of Altun Ha and Lamanai and dated as early as 2500 B.C., confirming an unbroken cultural lineage that is impressive by any civilization's standards. The area's vital trade routes, its abundant waterways, its access to the incomparable Caribbean, and its unique and fabulous natural treasures served as the catalyst for the rise of powerful Maya city states.

The emerald jungles of the Maya mountains yielded valuable medicinal herbs, plant materials, tropical hardwoods for building construction and ship-building, and plentiful wild game. Offshore, the world's second largest barrier reef throbbed with uncountable varieties of sea life, providing fertile fishing grounds for wide-ranging Maya fishing expeditions. Cities such as Lubaantun in the south served as markets and trading centers. With such bounty, the cities of Caracol and Xunantunich prospered, and some devoted their great wealth to the creation of powerful armies. One prominent example was Caracol, where in 562 A.D., after a six-year period of open hostilities, Caracol's warriors finally conquered the premier bastion of Maya power: the rival City of Tikal. Recently discovered glyphs document the momentous event with careful precision. The historical record further recounts that the Belizean Maya at times reigned supreme throughout the Guatemala/Belize lowland region.

In later centuries, this area has served as a magnet for opportunists and refugees. Runaway slaves, buccaneers turned entrepreneur, social misfits, and assorted modern-day adventurers all found the sparsely populated jungles, transparent coral reefs, unexplored underground caverns, and open-ended lifestyle much to their liking. As with the Maya of old, the rich natural legacy of Belize has continued to provide sustenance as well as paradise for the resourceful.

Caracol's armies, led by its supreme warlord Lord Water, defeated mighty Tikal in A.D. 562, usurping that city's political power and artistic culture for almost 150 years. Said to be larger than Tikal, Caracol is a classic period site containing a broad ceremonial area linked by extensive causeways to those in distant outlying areas that supplied the huge metropolis with its physical sustenance. This massive pyramid base is one of the 4,400 structures estimated to exist within Caracol's six-square-mile central core. (*Caracol*)

"El Castillo" at Xunantunich asserts its brooding presence over a nearby ceremonial plaza. Translated as "stone woman," Xunantunich is considered by some to be a religious center that celebrated the generative powers of life as expressed through the sexual symbolism contained within its sacred structures of pyramid, temple, and stelae. (*Xunantunich*)

This stucco frieze located on the side of a temple in Xunantunich contains
glyphs of an astronomical theme: the sun god, moon god, and the planet Venus.
(*Xunantunich*)

This is a large preclassic structure located in Lamanai, which means "submerged crocodile." The area contains numerous crocodile representations depicted in figurines, vessel decorations, and masks. Inhabited from the preclassic period to the seventeenth century, Lamanai overlooks a large lagoon that provided an excellent source of water. High-yield raised fields that attest to a program of intensive agriculture have been found in the area. Pollen studies show that maize was cultivated here as early as 1500 B.C. (*Lamanai*)

Lubaantun, which means "place of fallen stones," has eleven major structures distributed loosely about five major plazas. Settled after A.D. 700, a regional religious, political, administrative, and commercial center was established here. Lubaantun is best known as the origin of the famous Crystal Skull, unearthed by F. A. Mitchell-Hedges in 1926. This shattered pyramid is said to be the site of that spectacular discovery. (*Lubaantun*)

Lubaantun's crumbling temples fail to portray its important role as a regional market center where imported jade and obsidian would have been traded for local plant products, wild game, copal incense, maize, deep-water fish species from the nearby ocean, and locally abundant cacao beans, the universal currency of preconquest Mesoamerica. (*Lubaantun*)

CHICHÉN ITZÁ
TULUM

From the temple atop the Pyramid of Kukulcan, priests conducted numerous rituals, some of which are said to have included human sacrifice. In 1978, American archeologist Dennis Puleston was mysteriously struck dead by lightning while standing within the temple. Witnesses noted that he had recently handled ancient stone drums and effigies used to summon Chac, the god of rain, thunder, and lightning, from the underworld. (*Chichén Itzá*)

CHICHÉN ITZÁ LIES ON THE flat, dry northern Yucatan Peninsula. Early hunter-gatherers and fishermen populated this area as early as 8000 B.C. Like the peninsula itself, Chichén Itzá has experienced the comings and goings of many different groups of people over time. Consequently, its architecture reflects the physical and spiritual identities of its varied inhabitants.

Chichén Itzá and Cobá were the two largest cities in the northern Yucatan. According to legend, the Toltecs, an aggressive warrior tribe from northern Mexico, invaded Chichén Itzá and introduced their god Quetzalcoatl, who became known by the Maya as Kukulcan.

Temple artwork in Chichén Itzá depicts scenes of human sacrifice in relationship to the ball game. The largest ball court in the Americas exists here, 545 feet long. Painted images show members of the losing or winning team (archeologists aren't sure which) being beheaded. Physical evidence of human sacrifice victims associated with the ball game, however, has not been discovered or documented. Yet in the nearby *cenote*, a large sacred well, archeologists have recovered human skeletal remains and precious gold and jade objects.

Like any large and great city occupied by a diverse and sophisticated population, a full range of physical and spiritual activities made Chichén Itzá an exciting place to live. The city had nine ball courts, an advanced astronomical observatory, initiation schools for men and women, and huge residence halls. During the fall and spring equinoxes the feathered serpent made especially dramatic appearances. This astronomical event, rediscovered just ten years ago, attracts fifty to sixty thousand spectators each spring. At a certain moment, seven linked triangles align with a huge, sculptured serpent head at base of the El Castillo pyramid, giving the appearance of a great serpent undulating down the side of the pyramid. Accompanying ceremonies enabled participants to align their seven levels of human energy with the universal energies.

According to Hunbatz Men, "This unique geomantic event represents the manifestation of the sacred serpent of light (Kukulcan) entering into the physical world of matter. The serpent is worshiped by the Maya as a symbol of the cosmic synthesis of movement and measure. The sacred seven serves as a reminder of the galactic origins of Maya culture—the seven solar systems. At the moment the serpent arrives, we can feel the vibrations of Hunab K'U as the only giver of life. He comes to remind us of our destiny as cosmic beings heir to multidimensional realities far transcending our single-minded, three-dimensional physical world."

TULUM

Perched on a sandstone cliff overlooking a picture-postcard beach, the small and compact settlement of Tulum displays an understated human presence framed against a backdrop of powerful Mother Sea resplendent in all her glory. Tulum, like Chichén Itzá, manifests a strong Toltec influence. Yet the primary energy here is unmistakably the presence of nature. One is struck by the juxtaposition of sea and land: it is as if these elements intended to invite the human community into intimate communion with the natural forces, thus ensuring the continued fertility of all life.

Prior to the commencement of religious ceremonies, participants would deposit their offerings before the sacred serpents on the Platform of Eagles and Jaguars. (*Chichén Itzá*)

The Chichén Itzá ball court is the largest known ball court in the land of the Maya. The moving ball was seen to represent the motion of the living sun within the sky. (*Chichén Itzá*) ◀

In order to score, a team had to pass the ball through a special ring. Around the periphery of the ring two intertwined serpents depict the movement of the planets through the heavens. (*Chichén Itzá*)

In the Court of the Thousand Columns special teachers would prepare youths for their responsibilities in Chichén Itzá society as warriors and priests. (*Chichén Itzá*) ◀

Here in the old Maya section of Chichén Itzá in a temple called the Iglesia are seen several masks celebrating the rain god, Chac. Between the Chac masks are sculptures of the four Becabs—gods that represent the four directions and the basic elemental forces of earth, air, fire, and water. Also displayed is the sacred *G* or spiral symbolizing the Milky Way and the flow of the life force through all creation. (*Chichén Itzá*) ▶

In the Temple of the Warriors large columns and huge feathered serpent figures tower above a figure of a reposing Chac Mol, symbol of desire for enlightenment. This particularly dramatic setting served as an impressive temple receiving area to welcome initiates. (*Chichén Itzá*) ◄

This scuplture of a serpent head adorned with feathers and planetary symbols represents the teachings and responsibilities of becoming a Kukulcan or enlightened person. (*Chichén Itzá*) ►

A Chac Mol sits in the foreground. The Pyramid of Kukulcan stands in the background. (*Chichén Itzá*) ◄

The Caracol served as an astronomical observatory where Maya astronomers, using only their naked eyes, studied and documented the cyclical movements of the planets and performed precise calculations of the solar cycle. (*Chichén Itzá*)

A Toltec warrior has been carved on the Jaguar Platform at Chichén Itzá. Panels depicting eagles and jaguars devouring human hearts are also found here. (*Chichén Itzá*)

Skulls of captured enemies and sacrificial victims were displayed here on the *tzompantli* or skull platform. (*Chichén Itzá*) ▶

The Court of the Thousand Columns served as a training center for youths interested in studying the martial arts and the discipline of the will. (*Chichén Itzá*)

The Chac Mol holds a small bowl on his abdomen, possibly used for special offerings and heart sacrifices. (*Chichén Itzá*)

A sacred site that is home to the Diving God, Tulum is situated on a spectacular cliff overlooking transluscent waters. The Diving God represents the union of earth and sky, ocean and land. Tulum is oriented to the four cardinal directions, and certain buildings are aligned astronomically to mark solstice and equinox cycles. (*Tulum*)

The Temple of Venus is witness to the Maya and Toltec belief that, just as Venus returned from its eight-day sojourn in the underworld to rise again in the eastern sky along with the mighty sun, so too would human life undergo a parallel process of cyclic resurrection and rebirth. (*Tulum*) ▶

EPILOGUE

The Journey has just begun.
Seek the meaning of the sacred knowledge.
Seek the meaning of cycles within cycles.
The stones know.
They are the old ones who show the way.
They are the stones that speak.

This inscription portrays a
Maya ruler-priest, possibly
Chan Bahlum, explaining that
knowledge originates from
the Milky Way. In our solar
system the sun is the repre-
sentative of the Milky Way as
it channels powerful energies
from a distant galactic core
toward earth, influencing our
planetary evolution.
(*Palenque*)